FEAST OF THE
DRAGON

FEAST OF THE DRAGON

DRAGON

The Unofficial *House of the Dragon* and *Game of Thrones* Cookbook

By
Tom Grimm

With Photographs by
Tom Grimm & Dimitrie Harder

REEL
INK
PRESS

Dedicated to Thomas
"Uncle Tom" Stamm,
in gratitude and
friendship

CONTENTS

TO THIS (NEXT DISHES)

THEREAFTER

DRINKS

DINNER IS SERVED!

Game of Thrones is considered the most successful TV series of all time. Since 2019, when the last episode flickered on screens, fans have been eagerly awaiting a return to Westeros. And thanks to *House of the Dragon*, it's finally here!

House of the Dragon plays out 200 years before the events of *Game of Thrones* and tells of the rise and fall of the House of Targaryen. Like GoT, HBO's latest hit show is based on the work of Fantasy Maestro George R. R. Martin, who has always been very concerned about the physical welfare of his characters—at least until it is time to kill them off completely unexpectedly.

No question about it: George R. R. Martin is a connoisseur. In his works people eat, drink, and feast to their heart's content—even though he himself can't cook at all, as he admits. "All the pages in my books I've devoted to food over the years...all the lovingly embellished descriptions of the simplest and most exotic dishes...all those feasts that made your mouth water...I have never actually prepared even one of them!" His dishes are "made only of words": "Made of large, fleshy nouns and crispy verbs, well-seasoned with adjectives and adverbs." After all, his enthusiasm for food and drink runs like a (blood)red thread through Martin's emblematic work.

Fancy a taste? How about some of Sansa's Lemon Cake, Royal Cream Swans, Honeyed Locusts, a Bowl of Brown, or a hearty Breakfast on the Wall? All washed down with a powerful sip of Arbor Gold, of course!

From the imposing halls of King's Landing with their sumptuous delights, to the icy north with its warming, smoky fare, to the mysterious lands of Essos with its exotic eastern flavors—this culinary tour through the Seven Kingdoms will delight even the most discerning gourmands like Tyrion Lannister. And don't worry: As fantastic as the dishes gathered in this book may seem, the recipes are adapted so that even those unable to buy such bold ingredients as dragon peppers, camel meat, or live pigeons at the corner market can make a meal fit for a king!

But don't forget, dear reader, that all these recipes are ultimately nothing more than food for thought to stimulate your own creativity. After all, the greatest part of cooking is experimenting. And the same applies to the legendary world of Westeros as to the home kitchen: The only limits set are those of our own imagination!

Sincerely yours,

BREAKFAST

BREAKFAST ON THE WALL

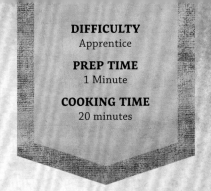

DIFFICULTY
Apprentice

PREP TIME
1 Minute

COOKING TIME
20 minutes

I. Put the cold eggs in a saucepan and pour in enough warm water so that the eggs float. Bring to a boil over medium heat and let the eggs simmer uncovered for 10 minutes. Then drain, rinse the eggs with as cold water as possible, and leave to cool.

II. In the meantime, melt the butter in a large nonstick skillet over medium heat. Add the steaks and sear on one side for 1 to 2 minutes. Then turn and sear the other side for 1 minute. Season to taste with pepper and smoked paprika and place briefly on a plate lined with paper towels to drain.

III. Peel the cooled eggs. Halve the hard-boiled eggs vertically and sprinkle with coarse sea salt to taste. Along with the steaks, serve some dried fruit (see Night's Watch Break Ration, page 23) and Night's Watch Black Bread (see page 19).

4 SERVINGS

4 cold eggs

1 tablespoon butter

4 slices Canadian bacon

Pepper, to taste

Smoked paprika, to taste

Coarse sea salt, to taste

Night's Watch Break Ration, if desired (see page 23)

Night's Watch Black Bread, to taste (see page 19)

OATBREAD

DIFFICULTY
Apprentice

PREP TIME
2 hours

COOKING TIME
10 to 12 minutes

I. Put the lukewarm water in a small bowl. Stir in the honey and crumble in the fresh yeast. Stir gently until the honey and yeast have completely dissolved and let rest for 10 minutes.

II. In the meantime, line two baking trays with parchment paper and dust with flour. Mix the flour and salt in a large bowl.

III. Add the yeast blend and knead for several minutes until forming a smooth, relatively firm dough. Cover with a clean tea towel and let rise in a warm place for about 60 minutes or until the dough has doubled in size.

IV. Knead the dough again after it has risen, divide into eight equal portions, and shape each into a ball on a lightly floured work surface. Using a wooden spoon handle, poke a hole in the center of each ball and then carefully enlarge the holes with your fingers to about 2 inches across.

V. Place the dough pieces on the prepared baking sheets, cover with clean tea towels, and let rise for 20 to 30 minutes. Meanwhile, preheat the oven to 450°F using top or bottom heat and bring the water for the brine to a boil in a bowl. As soon as the water boils, add the baking soda. Reduce the heat to simmer. Carefully put each piece of dough individually, one after the other, into the brine and turn after about 1 minute. After another 30 seconds, remove from the pot with a slotted spoon, place back on the baking sheet, sprinkle generously with oatmeal and sesame, and bake for 10 to 12 minutes. Oatbread is best eaten fresh!

8 PIECES

For the oatbread:

1 cup warm water

1 teaspoon honey

1⅗ tablespoon fresh yeast

4 cups pastry flour

2 level teaspoons salt

For the brine:

4¼ cups water

¼ cup baking soda

To sprinkle:

3.5 ounces fine oat flakes

1.5 ounces sesame seeds

APRICOT BUNS

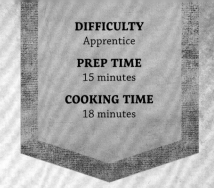

DIFFICULTY
Apprentice

PREP TIME
15 minutes

COOKING TIME
18 minutes

I. Preheat the oven to 395°F. Line a baking sheet with parchment paper.

II. Mix the flour, sugar, baking powder, orange zest, and salt in a large bowl.

III. Cut the butter into small cubes and mash in a small bowl using a fork. Add the cream cheese and mix thoroughly. Work in the apricots and the chocolate.

IV. In a mixing bowl, whisk together the egg, milk, and vanilla extract.

V. Combine the butter-apricot mixture and the egg-milk blend in the bowl with the flour and knead briefly with your hands until forming a dough. Divide the dough into two portions and shape each on a lightly floured surface into a round disc about 1¼ inches thick.

VI. Cut the discs into eight equal-sized "pie pieces" and place on the prepared baking sheet. Apply a little milk to the dough pieces with a pastry brush and bake for about 18 minutes. Make sure that the apricot buns don't get too dark, just golden!

16 BUNS

3¾ cups flour

½ cup sugar

2 heaping teaspoons baking powder

1 level teaspoon orange zest

1 pinch salt

4 ounces cold butter

8.5 ounces cream cheese

7.1 ounces dried apricots, roughly chopped

5.3 ounces white chocolate, roughly chopped

1 egg

¼ cup milk, plus more for brushing on

2 teaspoons vanilla extract

NIGHT'S WATCH BLACK BREAD

DIFFICULTY
Apprentice

PREP TIME
75 minutes
incl. resting time

COOKING TIME
120 minutes

I. Put the lukewarm water in a small bowl and dissolve the yeast in it.

II. Grease the loaf pan with butter.

III. In a large bowl, mix the spelt, rye groats, wholemeal flour, sunflower seeds, and salt.

IV. In a small saucepan, heat the buttermilk. Stir in the honey and apple butter. Pour into the bowl with the dry ingredients and mix. Add the yeast water and mix everything thoroughly. Pour into the prepared loaf pan, smooth the top, and let rest for 60 minutes.

V. In the meantime, preheat the oven to 300°F.

VI. Bake the bread for about 130 minutes. Let the loaf cool completely in the pan before turning it out onto a cutting board.

1 LOAF

3 tablespoons lukewarm water

1 heaping tablespoon fresh yeast

Butter for greasing the loaf pan

1⅖ cup spelt

2½ cups rye

1¾ cups wholemeal flour

1 cup sunflower seeds

2 teaspoons salt

2 cups buttermilk

1 teaspoon honey

1 tablespoon apple butter

Also needed:

Loaf pan (about 12-by-4-inch)

BLOODY BEET

DIFFICULTY
Apprentice

PREP TIME
5 minutes

COOKING TIME
25 minutes

I. Heat the coconut oil in a saucepan over medium heat. Add the onions, garlic, and ginger and sauté until translucent. Add the beetroot, mix together, and sauté for another 2 minutes.

II. Stir in the curry powder. Pour in the vegetable stock and beetroot juice and cook slowly for 10 minutes, stirring occasionally.

III. Add the tandoori paste, coconut milk, and lime juice to the pan and simmer for 5 to 6 minutes. Season with salt and pepper.

IV. Divide the soup between four serving bowls and garnish with a dollop of sour cream, if desired.

4 SERVINGS

2 tablespoons coconut oil

4.25 ounces onion, finely chopped

1 clove garlic, finely chopped

½ ounce ginger, freshly grated

17.5 ounces beetroot, precooked and julienned

2 tablespoons curry powder

1⅓ cups vegetable stock

2 cups beetroot juice

1 tablespoon tandoori paste

½ cup unsweetened coconut milk

2 tablespoons lime juice

Salt, pepper

Sour cream, for garnish

NIGHT'S WATCH BREAK RATION

DIFFICULTY
Apprentice

PREP TIME
10 minutes

DRYING TIME
5 to 15 hours

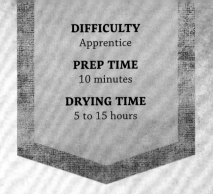

I. Peel, core, and cut the pears into thin slices. Peel, core, and cut the apples into thin slices. Core and halve the apricots. Core and halve the plums. Make sure the pieces of fruit are as large as possible so they dry evenly!

II. The easiest way to dry fruit is to use a dehydrator according to the device instructions. If you don't have one, you can just use your oven instead. Distribute the fruit on the sheets by type, leaving sufficient space in between (so the pieces don't touch each other) so the dried fruit can be removed sooner. Arrange the fruit so the cut surfaces face upward.

III. Place the trays in the oven with enough space between them to allow the air to circulate. Stick a wooden cooking spoon in the oven door so it is slightly ajar and the moist air can escape. The apples need 5 to 8 hours drying time, the pears a little longer. The plums and the apricots each need 10 to 15 hours drying time.

IV. The fruit is done drying when the pieces are leathery and pliable to the touch, and no longer excrete liquid if gently squeezed. Remove from the oven and let cool completely. Store dry in an airtight container. Can be kept for at least 6 months.

ABOUT 1⅓ POUNDS DRIED FRUIT

3.5 ounces pears

⅔ pound apples

3.5 ounces apricots

3.5 ounces plums

Also needed:

Dehydrator (optional)

HONEY CAKE

DIFFICULTY
Apprentice

PREP TIME
20 minutes

COOKING TIME
20 to 25 minutes

I. Combine the honey, butter, and brown sugar in a saucepan over medium heat, stirring constantly, until the sugar has completely dissolved. Remove from stove and let cool.

II. Preheat the oven to 350°F. Grease the muffin tin with butter and sprinkle with flour.

III. Whisk the eggs in a bowl. Add the honey-butter mixture and stir together.

IV. In a separate bowl, mix the flour, baking powder, gingerbread spice, and cinnamon thoroughly, then add to the wet ingredients. Mix everything together. Then fold in the dates, almonds, and chopped walnuts. Pour the dough into each cup, smooth the tops, and bake for 20 to 25 minutes. Remove and let cool completely in the mold.

V. Before serving, drizzle the honey cakes with a little honey and garnish each with a whole walnut.

12 CAKES

¼ cups honey, plus more for drizzling

3.5 ounces butter, plus more for the tin

¼ cup brown sugar

1 cup flour, plus more for the tin

2 eggs

1 teaspoon baking powder

1 teaspoon gingerbread spice mix

1 teaspoon cinnamon

2.5 ounces dates, very finely chopped

2.5 ounces ground almonds

Just over 2 ounces chopped walnuts

12 whole walnuts, for garnish

Also needed:

12-cup muffin tin

25

AT THE OUTSET

BOWL OF BROWN

DIFFICULTY
Apprentice

PREP TIME
5 minutes

COOKING TIME
50 minutes

I. Place the lentils in a bowl and wash with water. (No soaking necessary.)

II. Heat olive oil in a large saucepan, add the onions, and brown them. Add the ham and sauté for 1 to 2 minutes; then add the carrots, potatoes, lentils, bay leaf, and vegetable stock and simmer gently, with the lid on, over medium heat for about 40 to 45 minutes, or until the lentils are soft. If the stew is too thick, add some water.

III. In the meantime, sear the bacon on both sides in a pan with a little butter.

IV. When the lentils are finished, remove the bay leaf, stir in the vinegar (to taste) and season the stew with celery salt, pepper, and lovage. Serve on four deep plates and garnish each with a strip of bacon.

4 SERVINGS

1½ cups yellow lentils

1 to 2 tablespoons olive oil

1 large onion, finely chopped

3.5 ounces diced ham

2 carrots, finely diced

3 potatoes, finely diced

1 bay leaf

2½ cups vegetable stock

4 pieces fresh bacon

Some butter, for browning

2 to 3 tablespoons herb vinegar (to taste)

Celery salt, pepper, lovage (for seasoning)

TIP

Like all stews, this one tastes best when it has had the chance to sit, so if possible, serve it a day after preparation!

SWEET PUMPKIN SOUP

DIFFICULTY
Apprentice

PREP TIME
10 minutes

COOKING TIME
50 minutes

I. Preheat the oven to 200°F. Line a baking sheet with parchment paper.

II. Wash and quarter the pumpkin.

III. Using a tablespoon, carefully scrape out the seeds and threads and discard. Chop the pumpkin into chunks, including the skin, place on the baking sheet, and bake for 20 minutes. Remove the tray and pour out the excess liquid.

IV. In a large saucepan over medium-high heat, melt the butter. Sauté the shallots and garlic until translucent. Add the pumpkin pieces and sauté briefly. Add the potatoes and carrots, then add the paprika and flour and mix everything together. Pour in the vegetable broth, white wine, and coconut milk. Bring to boil briefly, then reduce the heat and simmer, covered, for about 25 minutes, occasionally stirring.

V. Add the ginger and curry powder. Finely purée the soup in a saucepan using an immersion blender, add the cream, and season generously with salt and pepper. Garnish with roasted pumpkin seeds to serve.

4 TO 6 SERVINGS

1 medium-sized Hokkaido pumpkin (about 3.25 pounds)

2 tablespoons butter

2 shallots, finely chopped

1 garlic clove, finely chopped

7 ounces potatoes, diced

1 teaspoon noble sweet paprika

2 tablespoons flour

1 carrot, finely grated

3⅓ cups vegetable broth

⅘ cup white wine

½ cup coconut milk

¾-inch fresh ginger, finely grated

3 tablespoons curry powder

1.8 ounces whipping cream

Salt, pepper

Roasted pumpkin seeds, for garnish

TIP

The white wine can easily be omitted from this recipe. However, you should add a splash of vinegar instead to give the soup a certain acidity.

CERSEI'S BITTER GREENS SALAD

DIFFICULTY
Apprentice

PREP TIME
5 minutes
PREPARATION
5 minutes

I. Wash the apple, peel, core, and cut into slices.

II. Place the balsamic vinegar, honey, red pepper jam, lime juice, and olive oil in a small, sealable container and shake vigorously to mix well. Chill in the refrigerator until ready to serve. Shake well before using.

III. In a salad bowl, combine the salad mix with the apple slices, dragon fruit, and pine nuts. Pour the dressing over the salad and toss thoroughly to fully coat. Serve immediately.

2 TO 3 SERVINGS

1 green apple

¾ cup balsamic vinegar

3 tablespoons honey

2 tablespoons red pepper jam

2 tablespoons lime juice

1 tablespoon olive oil

7 ounces mixed dark bitter greens (e.g., arugula, kale, radicchio)

1 dragon fruit, thinly sliced

1.75 ounces pine nuts

BRAAVOS MUSSELS & SCALLOPS

DIFFICULTY
Apprentice

PREP TIME
10 minutes +
2 hours cooling time

COOKING TIME
45 minutes

To prepare the garlic chili mussels:

I. In a large saucepan, heat the vegetable oil over medium-high heat. Add the garlic and shallots and sauté until translucent. Deglaze with the white wine and let reduce 2 to 3 minutes.

II. Add the vegetable stock, water, tomatoes, mirepoix, sherry, vegetable bouillon, pepper, cream, and celery salt to the pot. Bring to boil, stirring regularly.

III. Add the thawed mussels to the broth along with the chili rings and let simmer for 12 to 15 minutes. Always discard the mussels that didn't open during cooking!

Prepare the scallops in herb butter:

IV. Wash the herbs, shake dry, and finely chop.

V. Put the herbs, garlic, and butter in a small bowl and, using a fork, mix well. Season to taste with salt, cover with plastic wrap and chill in the fridge for at least 2 hours before use. Keeps well refrigerated for up to 2 weeks.

VI. When the herb butter is ready, preheat the oven to 300°F and line a baking sheet with parchment paper.

VII. Pat the mussels dry with paper towels, arrange them in their shells on the baking sheet, and lightly season with salt and pepper. Then put a dab of herb butter in the middle of each mussel and cook in the preheated oven for 5 to 6 minutes. Remove from the oven, let cool briefly, and enjoy while warm!

4 TO 6 SERVINGS

For the garlic chili mussels:

1 tablespoon vegetable oil

4 cloves garlic, finely chopped

2 shallots, finely chopped

Just under ½ cup white wine

Just over 2 cups vegetable stock

Just over 2 cups water

14 ounces plum tomatoes (jar/can)

1 serving mirepoix mix, finely chopped

¼ cup sherry (medium dry)

1 tablespoon vegetable stock bouillon

1 teaspoon black pepper

½ cup culinary cream

1 teaspoon celery salt

4.5 pounds frozen mussels, ready to cook, thawed

½ red chili pepper, cut into thin rings

For the scallops in herb butter:

1 bunch fresh herbs (e.g., parsley, basil, chives, chervil)

1 clove garlic, very finely chopped

1 cup plus 2 tablespoons softened butter

Salt

24 frozen scallops with shells

Pepper

COLD FRUIT SOUP

DIFFICULTY
Apprentice

PREP TIME
5 minutes

COOKING TIME
10 minutes

I. Pour the apple juice into a medium-sized pot. Remove 5 tablespoons of juice and stir together with the sugar, vanilla extract, and cornstarch in a small container until smooth.

II. Add the berries and fruit to the pot with the apple juice and bring to a boil. Allow to boil briefly and then stir in the cornstarch mixture.

III. Let simmer for 5 to 6 minutes, stirring regularly. Remove from the stove. Let the soup cool for a few minutes and then chill in the refrigerator until ready to serve. Garnish with a sprig of fresh mint, if desired.

4 SERVINGS

1¾ cups apple juice

2 tablespoons sugar

1 teaspoon vanilla extract

1 tablespoon cornstarch

1 pound berries and fruits (e.g., raspberries, blackberries, blueberries, cherries)

Fresh mint, for garnish

WINTERFELL VINEGAR MUSHROOMS

DIFFICULTY
Apprentice

PREP TIME
10 minutes

COOKING TIME
20 minutes

I. Clean the mushrooms and cut, as desired, into slices, quarters, or pieces.

II. Melt the butter in a large, nonstick skillet over medium heat. Add the shallots and garlic and sauté until translucent. Add the carrots and leek and sauté briefly. Add the mushrooms to the pan, season generously with pepper, and simmer uncovered for 5 to 6 minutes.

III. Meanwhile, in a small bowl, whisk together the balsamic vinegar, soy sauce, honey, and mustard.

IV. Once the mushrooms have released most of their liquid, stir in the vinegar mixture. Add the thyme and let simmer gently, stirring occasionally, until the carrots are ready. Fold in the chopped parsley right before serving.

2 SERVINGS

1 pound mixed fresh mushrooms

1 tablespoon butter

2 shallots, finely chopped

2 tablespoons garlic, finely chopped

2 carrots, roughly sliced

½ leek, cut into thin rings

Pepper

¼ cup balsamic vinegar

¼ cup soy sauce

2 tablespoons honey

2 tablespoons mustard

3 sprigs thyme

2 tablespoons fresh parsley, finely chopped

CREAM OF MUSHROOM SOUP WITH SNAILS

DIFFICULTY
Apprentice

PREP TIME
10 minutes

COOKING TIME
50 minutes

I. In a saucepan over medium heat, melt the butter. Add the onion and leek and sauté for 2 to 3 minutes. Then add the mushrooms and sauté lightly on all sides (2 to 3 minutes). Deglaze with vegetable stock. Add the celery stalk (whole) and thyme, reduce the heat, and simmer uncovered for about 40 minutes.

II. Remove the thyme and celery and purée the soup in the pot with an immersion blender. Season with salt and pepper. Stir in the sour cream.

III. Rinse the snails with fresh water, pat dry with paper towels, and leave to soak in the hot soup for 3 to 4 minutes before serving. Never cook! Garnish with a sprig of curly parsley and enjoy warm

4 SERVINGS

1 tablespoon butter

1 onion, finely chopped

1 leek, cut into thin rings

1.5 pounds mixed fresh mushrooms, cut into pieces

34 ounces vegetable stock

1 celery stalk

1 thyme sprig

Salt

Freshly ground black pepper

2 tablespoons sour cream

5.25 ounces snails (canned), drained

Some curly parsley, for garnish

PORK RILLETTES

DIFFICULTY
Scholar

PREP TIME
15 minutes

PREPARATION
5 1/2 hours

I. Finely grind the coriander seeds using a mortar.

II. Preheat the oven to 300°F.

III. Heat the lard in a casserole dish. Sauté the shallots and garlic over medium heat. Add the meat and lightly brown, stirring regularly, for about 6 to 8 minutes. Add the coriander seeds, season with salt and pepper and deglaze with the veal stock. Add the bay leaves. Press the juniper berries lightly with the flat side of a knife and add to the pot together with the marjoram, thyme, and rosemary. Pour in enough water to cover the meat completely. Briefly bring to a boil, cover, and then gently stew in the oven on the lowest rack for 4 1/2 to 5 hours. In the end, the meat has to be so tender that it falls apart on its own.

IV. Strain the meat in a sieve and catch the broth. Once drained, place the meat in a large bowl. Remove and discard the bay leaves and juniper berries. Using two forks, shred the meat. Use a tablespoon to skim off 6 to 8 tablespoons of fat from the saved broth and mix in with the meat. If possible, do not use more fat, otherwise the rillettes will become too solid! Season the meat generously with salt and pepper.

V. Place the meat in the prepared, sterilized mason jars and press down firmly until there are no more air pockets. To do this, gently tap the bottom of the glass jar several times on the work surface. Skim off some of the fat from the broth and spread it in the glasses so that the meat is completely covered. Let cool completely, then close the jars. Serve with Night's Watch Black Bread, if desired (see page 19).

MAKES 6 SMALL JARS (7 OUNCES EACH)

2 teaspoons coriander seeds

4.25 ounces lard

3 ounces shallots, finely diced

2 cloves garlic, finely diced

21.25 ounces pork belly, cut into about 1.5-inch cubes

1.3 pounds pork shoulder, cut into about 1.5-inch cubes

Salt, pepper

Just over 2 cups veal stock

2 bay leaves

3 juniper berries

3 sprigs marjoram, finely plucked

5 sprigs thyme, finely plucked

2 sprigs rosemary, finely plucked

Also needed:

6 boiled jars with lids
(each with a capacity of 7 ounces)

ONION SOUP

DIFFICULTY
Apprentice

PREP TIME
5 minutes

COOKING TIME
40 minutes

I. Rinse the thyme, dry it, and pluck the leaves.

II. In a large saucepan over high heat, melt the clarified butter. Add the onions and sauté until translucent, 5 to 8 minutes, stirring occasionally. Then reduce the heat, add the garlic, and sweat briefly. Stir in the thyme, bay leaf, and sugar, pour in the vegetable stock and white wine, and simmer gently for 30 minutes.

III. Season the soup with salt and pepper to taste, divide into deep plates or bowls, and garnish with a little fresh parsley. Best served with Night's Watch Black Bread (see page 19).

5 TO 6 SERVINGS

5 sprigs thyme

3 tablespoons clarified butter

2.25 pounds onions, roughly chopped

7 ounces red onions, cut into thin rings

4 garlic cloves, finely chopped

1 bay leaf

1 tablespoon cane sugar

4 ¼ cups vegetable stock

1 ¼ cups white wine

Salt

Freshly ground black pepper

Fresh parsley, for garnish

MAIN COURSES

MUTTON IN ONION-AND-BEER STEW

DIFFICULTY
Scholar

PREP TIME
10 minutes

COOKING TIME
2 hours,
15 minutes

I. Heat the olive oil in a skillet over medium heat. Generously salt and pepper the lamb shoulders all over and sear on all sides for 3 to 4 minutes. Remove from the pan and set aside.

II. Preheat the oven, using the convection setting, to 300°F.

III. Brown the onion in the roasting pan. Add the garlic and sweat briefly. Then add the carrots and celeriac, mix well, and brown the vegetables on all sides for a few minutes. Put the meat back in the roasting pan and deglaze with the beer.

IV. Put the roasting pan in the preheated oven and braise for 2 hours. Turn every 20 minutes and pour in a little of the lamb stock. As soon as the meat is cooked, remove from the roasting pan; then, before cutting, drain and let rest for 5 minutes.

V. Meanwhile, mix the lemon zest and freshly chopped parsley into the stew and serve with the roast lamb. If the stock is too runny, thicken with a little cornstarch mixture if necessary.

4 TO 5 SERVINGS

3 tablespoons olive oil

Salt, pepper

2 lamb shoulders, lean and without bones (about 1.5 pounds each)

4 large onions, cut into thin rings

3 garlic cloves, finely chopped

2 carrots, finely chopped

½ a small celeriac, finely chopped

Just over 2 cups dark beer

Just over 2 cups lamb stock

Zest of ½ organic lemon

Fresh parsley, finely chopped

Sauce thickener (optional)

TIP

Since the alcohol in the beer boils off, children also can enjoy this dish! Alternatively, simply use malt beer.

FREY PIE

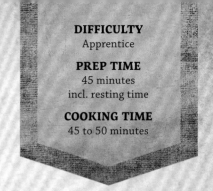

DIFFICULTY
Apprentice

PREP TIME
45 minutes
incl. resting time

COOKING TIME
45 to 50 minutes

I. Heat the olive oil in a large saucepan. Add the onion and sauté until translucent. Add the ham and sauté. Add the ground meat and sear until hot, stirring occasionally. Season the meat with salt, pepper, and nutmeg. Add the carrots, rutabaga, mushrooms, oregano, and rosemary. Cook for 3 minutes. Remove from the stove and set aside.

II. Melt the butter in a small saucepan and stir in the flour with a whisk. Add the beef stock to the pan with the ground meat and simmer uncovered until there is hardly any liquid left.

III. Preheat the oven to 325°F.

IV. For the shortcrust pastry, knead all the ingredients together thoroughly in a bowl and place in the fridge, covered with plastic wrap, for 30 minutes. Then roll out ⅔ of the dough on a work surface lightly sprinkled with flour to a thickness of about $1/10$ of an inch. Line a springform pan (7 inches across) with the dough. Press the dough lightly around the edges of the springform pan, letting it overhang at the top.

V. Place the filling into the springform pan and smooth it out. Roll out the remaining dough so that it fits the diameter of the springform pan. Cover the filling, keeping it flush, press down a little, and fold over the dough that protrudes at the edges. Brush with the beaten egg, cut a cross shape into the top with a knife, and bake the pastry in the preheated oven for about 45 to 50 minutes. Let rest for 5 minutes before serving.

1 PIE (ABOUT 4 SERVINGS)

For the pie filling:

1 to 2 tablespoon olive oil, for sautéing

1 onion, finely diced

3.5 ounces diced ham

1.5 pounds mixed ground meat (beef and pork)

Salt, pepper

1 teaspoon nutmeg, freshly ground

2 carrots, finely diced

3.5 ounces rutabaga, finely diced

4.5 ounces button mushrooms, quartered

½ teaspoon oregano

½ teaspoon rosemary

3 heaping tablespoon butter

3¾ tablespoons flour

⅘ cup beef stock

Egg, beaten

For the shortcrust:

1 cup cold butter, cubed

1¾ heaping cups flour

1 tablespoon sugar

1 teaspoon salt

½ cup buttermilk

Also needed:
Springform pan
(about 7 inches across)

HOUSE LANNISTER GOLDEN ROAST

DIFFICULTY
Apprentice

PREP TIME
5 minutes

COOKING TIME
2 hours

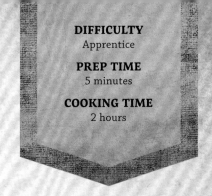

I. Preheat the oven, using the convection setting, to 350°F. Line a baking sheet with a large piece of aluminum foil.

II. In a bowl, combine the shallots, garlic, mustard, horseradish, marjoram, turmeric, pepper, saffron threads, and sea salt.

III. Heat the olive oil in a nonstick pan over medium heat and sear the roast pork on all sides. Then place the roast in the middle of the aluminum foil on the baking sheet and generously coat all sides with the marinade. Wrap in the aluminum foil and cook for about 2 hours; brush with more marinade every 20 minutes.

IV. Remove from the oven, let rest in the foil for a few minutes, then slice and serve.

4 SERVINGS

2 shallots, finely chopped

1 garlic clove, finely chopped

8 tablespoons mustard (medium heat)

2 tablespoons grated horseradish

1 tablespoon marjoram

1 tablespoon turmeric

1 tablespoon black pepper

1 pinch saffron threads

1 tablespoon sea salt

2 tablespoons olive oil

1 pork loin roast (about 2 pounds)

ROYAL BOAR RIBS

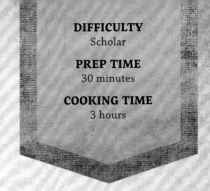

DIFFICULTY
Scholar

PREP TIME
30 minutes

COOKING TIME
3 hours

I. Heat the olive oil in a small saucepan over medium heat. Add the shallots and garlic and sweat until translucent. Add the curry paste, ketchup, beer, Worcestershire sauce, molasses, and apple cider vinegar, mix well, and simmer for 25 minutes, stirring occasionally, to noticeably reduce. Finely purée in the saucepan using an immersion blender.

II. Preheat the oven, using the convection setting, to 275°F.

III. Line a baking sheet with parchment paper and place a broiler pan on top.

IV. Place the ribs, meat side down, on the grid, season generously with salt and pepper, and brush fully with the spice blend. Place on the oven's middle rack and let simmer for about 3 hours; turn regularly (at least every 20 minutes), coating with the juices.

V. When the ribs are done, turn the oven off and let the ribs rest in the oven for a few minutes. Then cut open the aluminum foil, arrange the ribs on a large plate with grapes and cheese cubes, and serve immediately.

4 TO 6 SERVINGS

1 tablespoon olive oil

2 shallots, finely chopped

1 garlic clove, finely chopped

2 teaspoons red curry paste

½ cup ketchup

1¼ cups beer or malt beer

2 tablespoons Worcestershire sauce

2 tablespoons molasses

1 tablespoon apple cider vinegar

3 pounds pork rib rack

Salt, pepper

Grapes, for garnish

Cheese cubes, for garnish

TIP

Since the alcohol in the beer boils off, children also can enjoy these ribs! Alternatively, just use malt beer.

PEA SOUP

DIFFICULTY
Apprentice

PREP TIME
10 minutes

COOKING TIME
45 minutes

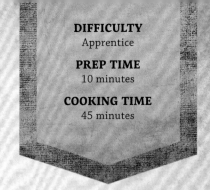

I. In a large pot, melt the lard over medium-high heat. Sauté the onions until translucent. Add the mirepoix and sweat. After 2 to 3 minutes add the cured pork collar, then after another 2 to 3 minutes, add the potatoes. Deglaze with the vegetable stock, pour in the water, and stir in the peas. Simmer uncovered for 30 minutes.

II. Meanwhile, fry the bacon slices in a nonstick pan with a little butter over medium heat until crispy (2 to 3 minutes per side). To drain, transfer to a plate lined with paper towels and cover loosely with aluminum foil to keep warm.

III. Coarsely mash the soup with a potato masher. Season to taste with pepper, celery salt, lovage, marjoram, and apple cider vinegar. Spread on soup plates and serve with the bacon.

6 TO 8 SERVINGS

1 tablespoon lard

2 onions, finely chopped

1 serving of soup vegetables (celery, carrot, leek)/mirepoix, finely chopped

10.5 ounces cured pork (such as bacon or Canadian bacon), cubed

4 medium potatoes (floury), peeled and finely diced

4¼ cups vegetable stock

Just over 2 cups water

1.75 pounds frozen peas

Some butter for browning

Bacon, thickly sliced, to taste

Pepper, celery salt, lovage, marjoram, to taste

1 tablespoon apple cider vinegar

TIP

Like most soups, this one tastes especially delicious when properly steeped. So it's best to prepare the night before and warm it up the next day to serve!

RACK OF LAMB WITH BRAISED VEGETABLES

DIFFICULTY
Scholar

PREP TIME
15 minutes

COOKING TIME
60 minutes

I. Preheat the oven to 355°F.

II. Peel and halve the garlic cloves and shallots. Peel the carrots, parsley roots, and potatoes and cut them in half or into smaller pieces, depending on the size. Wash the celery, destring, and cut into pieces. Wash, trim, and cut the peppers into pieces.

III. In a saucepan over medium heat, heat 2 tablespoons olive oil. Sauté the prepared vegetables for 6 to 8 minutes. Generously season with salt and pepper. Pour in the stock, spread in a baking dish, and roast for 30 minutes.

IV. In the meantime, rinse the herbs, shake dry, and pluck off the leaves. Then, in a blender, finely mince the herbs and bread cubes. Season the rack of lamb with salt and pepper and sear on all sides in a nonstick pan with the rest of the olive oil (4 to 5 minutes).

V. Place the meat on top of the vegetables in the baking dish and cover generously with the herb crumbs. Spread the butter in small pats on top. Return to the oven for about 15 minutes.

VI. Divide the rack of lamb into chops as desired and serve with the vegetables.

4 SERVINGS

2 garlic cloves

6 shallots

4 small carrots

3 parsley roots

12 small potatoes

3 sticks celery

1 red bell pepper

1 yellow pepper

4 tablespoons olive oil

Salt, pepper

⅘ cup chicken stock

1 sprig each parsley, thyme, and rosemary

1 slice white bread, finely diced

2 racks lamb (about 14 ounces)

2⅛ tablespoons butter

ALMOND-CRUSTED TROUT

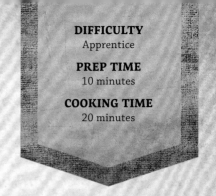

DIFFICULTY
Apprentice

PREP TIME
10 minutes

COOKING TIME
20 minutes

I. Preheat the oven, using the convection setting, to 400°F. Line a baking sheet with parchment paper.

II. Rinse the trout under cold running water; clean the abdominal cavity well. Pat dry with paper towels. Season vigorously inside and out with salt and pepper.

III. Rinse the lemon with hot water and dry. Cut slightly more than half the lemon into very thin slices; squeeze out the rest.

IV. Cover the trout evenly with the lemon slices and with ¾ of the chopped parsley.

V. Melt the butter in a heat-resistant bowl in the microwave and mix in the lemon juice. Brush the trout generously with it, place the fish on the baking sheet, and cook in the preheated oven for 6 to 8 minutes. Then turn, brush again with the lemon butter, sprinkle evenly with the sliced almonds, and cook for another 10 minutes. Finally, remove from the oven, brush with the remaining lemon butter, sprinkle with the leftover chopped parsley, and serve hot.

4 SERVINGS

4 trout (about 13.25 ounces each), ready to cook

Salt, pepper

1 organic lemon

½ bunch parsley, finely chopped

½ cup butter

4 tablespoons sliced almonds

TYRION'S FAVORITE LEG OF LAMB

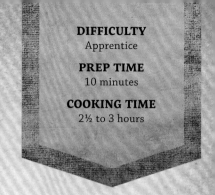

DIFFICULTY
Apprentice

PREP TIME
10 minutes

COOKING TIME
2½ to 3 hours

I. Rinse the lamb under cold water, pat dry with paper towels, and remove skin and tendons with a sharp knife. Generously salt and pepper all over.

II. Use the flat side of a knife blade to lightly crush the unpeeled garlic cloves.

III. Preheat the oven, using the convection setting, to 300°F.

IV. In a large roasting pan over medium heat, heat the olive oil. Add the leg of lamb and brown on all sides (5 to 6 minutes). Remove from the roasting pan and set aside.

V. Put the onions in the roasting pan and sauté until translucent. Then add the garlic, carrots, and celery and sauté, stirring regularly. Add the tomato paste, thyme, and rosemary and sauté briefly. Then pour in the grape juice and lamb stock and let boil for 10 minutes.

VI. Place the lamb on the vegetables in the roasting pan so that the meat is almost completely covered with liquid and bring boil briefly. Then place the roasting pan on the second rack of the oven for about 120 to 150 minutes or until the meat is wonderfully soft and tender. Then turn off the oven, remove from the roasting pan, wrap in aluminum foil, and keep warm in the oven.

VII. Pour the roast drippings from the roasting pan into a small saucepan through a sieve. Press and discard the vegetables. In a mug, stir the cornstarch with a bit of water until smooth, add to the saucepan, and bring to boil while stirring constantly so the sauce thickens.

VIII. To serve, place the lamb on a serving plate, garnish with pine nuts, and serve with the sauce.

4 SERVINGS

1 lamb leg
(about 3.25 lbs.)

Salt, pepper

4 cloves garlic, unpeeled

4 tablespoons olive oil

3 large onions, finely diced

4 carrots, finely diced

2 celery sticks, finely diced

3 teaspoons tomato paste

3 sprigs thyme

2 sprigs rosemary

½ cup red grape juice

4 cups lamb stock

2 teaspoons cornstarch

Some water

Pine nuts, for garnish

DORNISH QUAILS

DIFFICULTY
Scholar

PREP time
10 minutes

COOKING TIME
90 minutes

I. Place the sugar in a saucepan over medium heat and caramelize until golden brown. Then add ¼ cup butter, add the shallots, and sauté until translucent. Pour in 1 cup chicken stock and lightly salt and pepper. Put the lid on, reduce the heat, and simmer gently for 20 minutes. Then remove the lid and simmer for another 30 minutes until syrupy. Stir in the lemon juice. Pour the pot's contents into the casserole dish. Add the apricots and tomatoes and mix well.

II. Preheat the oven, using the convection setting, to 390°F.

III. Press the cardamom pods lightly. Cut the orange into sixteen small pieces. Stuff each quail with two cardamom pods, two pieces of orange, and half a bay leaf. Tie the quail legs together with kitchen twine.

IV. In a small heat-resistant bowl, melt the remaining butter and mix with the honey. Brush the quail all over and place in the casserole dish. Add the remaining stock and cook on the bottom oven rack for 20 minutes.

V. Rinse the mint, shake dry, and pluck off the leaves.

VI. In the meantime, prepare the couscous according to the packet instructions.

VII. As soon as the quails are done, take them out of the casserole dish. Add the couscous and mix everything carefully. Then spread the fruit couscous over flat plates, put two quail on each, and garnish with the mint and pomegranate seeds.

4 SERVINGS

- ½ cup sugar
- ½ cup butter
- 10.5 ounces shallots, finely chopped
- 1¾ cups chicken stock
- Salt
- Freshly ground black pepper
- 2 tablespoons lemon juice
- 1.75 ounces dried apricots
- 0.75 ounces dried tomatoes
- 16 green cardamom pods
- 1 small organic orange
- 8 quails (about 6.5 ounces each), ready to cook
- 4 bay leaves
- 4 tablespoons lavender honey
- 1 sprig mint
- 1¼ cups couscous
- Pomegranate seeds, for garnish

Also needed:

Kitchen twine

Casserole dish
(about 8.75 inch by 7.75 inch)

OLD NAN'S KIDNEY PIE

DIFFICULTY
Apprentice

PREP TIME
15 minutes

COOKING TIME
3 hours
incl. resting time

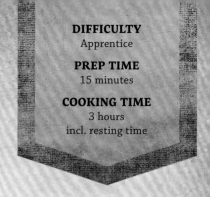

I. Rinse the beef kidneys with cold water and pat dry with paper towels. Use a sharp knife to remove the membrane surrounding the kidney if you haven't already. Remove tendons and fat. Finely dice the meat.

II. Sift the flour into a bowl and make a well in the middle. Put the butter pats, 1 tablespoon salt, eggs, and 2 tablespoons water in the depression and quickly knead into a smooth dough. Wrap in plastic wrap and put in the refrigerator for 2 hours.

III. Heat the olive oil in a pan over medium heat. Add the onions and sweat until translucent. Add the meat and sear on all sides. Add the mushrooms, carrots, and celery, mix well, and sauté for another 8 to 10 minutes.

IV. Meanwhile, wash the thyme and shake dry. Pluck off the leaves and add to the pan. Pour in the beef stock and simmer uncovered for 8 to 10 minutes. Season with salt and pepper.

V. Preheat the oven, using the convection setting, to 350°F.

VI. Remove the dough from the fridge and divide into three equal portions. Roll out two of the portions on a lightly floured work surface and use them to line the pie cases. Spread the filling evenly among the molds and fill to just below the top edge. Roll out the remaining dough and cut out or punch out circles that are slightly larger than the molds. Place a circle of dough on each pie and poke a few holes in it with a fork.

VII. In a cup, mix the egg yolk with a bit of water and brush the tops of the pies with it. Bake for 25 minutes. Sprinkle the pies with a little cheddar and bake for another 5 minutes. Carefully remove the pies from the molds, garnish with a little fresh parsley, if desired, and serve warm.

8 PIES

1 beef kidney (or 17.5 ounces ground beef)

3 heaping cups wholemeal spelt flour

8 ounces yogurt butter spread, in pats

Salt

2 eggs

2 tablespoons water, plus extra

1 tablespoon olive oil

2 onions, finely chopped

9 ounces mushrooms, thinly sliced

2 carrots, finely diced

1 stick of celery, finely diced

3 sprigs thyme

1 cup beef stock

Pepper

1 egg yolk

Grated cheddar cheese, to taste

Fresh parsley, as garnish

Also needed:

8 pie molds (about 4 inches across)

SUNSPEAR TAGINE

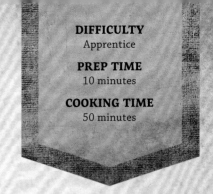

DIFFICULTY
Apprentice

PREP TIME
10 minutes

COOKING TIME
50 minutes

I. In a bowl, mix 1 tablespoon of olive oil, the tomato paste, and the harissa with the pepper and salt.

II. Rinse the chicken thighs in cold water, pat dry with paper towels, and brush generously with the harissa spice mixture.

III. Heat 2 tablespoons olive oil in a deep pan over medium heat. Sauté the onion, garlic, and ginger for 2 to 3 minutes. Add the chicken thighs and sear briefly on all sides. Add the apricots, chickpeas, lentils, pomegranate seeds, raisins, and cinnamon stick and mix well. Pour in the vegetable stock and orange juice and bring to boil, stirring regularly. Stir in the lemon juice, put the lid on, and let simmer for 20 minutes. Then remove the lid and cook uncovered for another 20 minutes.

IV. Just before serving, stir in the cilantro. Remove and discard the cinnamon stick.

4 SERVINGS

3 tablespoons olive oil

3 tablespoons tomato paste

½ teaspoon harissa (spice paste)

1 teaspoon pepper

1 teaspoon salt

8 chicken legs

2 red onions, finely diced

2 garlic cloves, finely diced

1 piece fresh ginger
(about 1.25 inches), finely chopped

6 dried apricots, roughly chopped

3.5 ounces chickpeas (canned), drained

3.5 ounces yellow lentils (canned), drained

4 tablespoons pomegranate seeds

3 tablespoons raisins

1 cinnamon stick

⅘ cup vegetable stock

½ cup orange juice

Juice from ½ organic lemon

2 sprigs cilantro, finely chopped

Also needed:

Tagine pot (optional), or another deep pan

TIP

If you use a tagine to prepare this dish, follow the same process as you would with the pan, except that the lid of the clay pot stays on the entire time!

TYWIN LANNISTER'S OXTAIL STEW

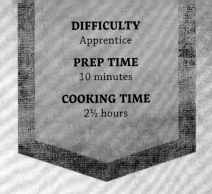

DIFFICULTY
Apprentice

PREP TIME
10 minutes

COOKING TIME
2½ hours

I. Have the butcher cut the oxtail into finger-length pieces or chop it yourself.

II. If you want to serve the soup in bread bowls, carefully hollow the loaves so that the bottom and sides of the crust remain intact.

III. Melt half the butter in a large saucepan over medium heat. Add the onions and sauté until translucent. Remove the onions and set aside. Put the oxtail pieces into the pan and brown vigorously on all sides (5 to 6 minutes). Add the soup greens and the bay leaves and roast briefly. Add the onions back in. Fill with water, lightly salt, and simmer for 90 to 120 minutes or until the meat can be easily removed from the bone. Then remove the oxtail pieces and shred the meat. Strain the broth through a sieve into a clean container.

IV. Rinse the saucepan and melt the remaining butter over medium heat. Add the flour, mix well, and let dry. Then add the beef broth, one ladle at a time, and stir until smooth again. Pour the remaining stock into the pot and season with salt, paprika, pepper, and a pinch of sugar. Pour in the red wine and add the oxtail meat to the soup. Let simmer for 10 minutes.

V. Meanwhile, cook the tagliatelle in a saucepan of heavily salted water, according to the package instructions. Then drain carefully, add to the soup, mix everything together, and serve in the bread bowls or in soup bowls.

4 SERVINGS

1 pound oxtail

4 tablespoons butter

2 onions, finely chopped

½ bunch soup greens (e.g., celery, leek, parsley), finely chopped

2 bay leaves

6⅓ cups water

Salt

3 tablespoons flour

1 teaspoon paprika

Pepper

1 pinch sugar

1 cup red wine (dry)

9 ounces tagliatelle

Also needed:

Solid small round loaves for bread bowls (optional)

DORNISH "SNAKE" WITH FIERY SAUCE

DIFFICULTY
Apprentice

PREP TIME
5 minutes

RESTING TIME
1 hour

I. Mix the salsa, chili sauce, roasted red pepper sauce, and red chili paste (depending on how hot you want the sauce) in a small bowl.

II. Add the shallot and garlic and mix well. Cover loosely with plastic wrap and leave in the fridge for at least 1 hour. Stir thoroughly again before serving.

III. Serve with the eel.

2 TO 3 SERVINGS

For the fiery sauce:

5 tablespoons salsa of choice

5 tablespoons chili sauce

2 tablespoons roasted red pepper sauce

1 to 2 tablespoons hot sauce, to taste

½ shallot, finely chopped

1 clove garlic, finely pressed

1 smoked eel (⅔ pound), ready to cook

BENJEN STARK'S ELK MEATBALLS

DIFFICULTY
Apprentice

PREP time
10 minutes

COOKING TIME
25 minutes

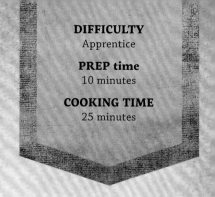

I. Using a mortar and pestle, grind the activated charcoal into a fine powder. Alternatively, put the tablets in a freezer bag, place them on the work surface, and crumble finely.

II. Put the ground meat, breadcrumbs, egg, shallot, and mustard in a bowl with the charcoal powder, season as desired with salt, pepper, and nutmeg and knead everything thoroughly. With slightly moistened hands, form golf ball-sized balls from the meat mixture.

III. Melt the butter in a large pan at medium heat and brown the meatballs on all sides until golden (about 5 minutes). Then remove from the pan, place on a plate lined with paper towels to drain, and cover loosely with aluminum foil. If necessary, keep warm in a preheated oven at 125°F while you prepare the sauce.

IV. For the sauce, fry the onions vigorously in the fat remaining in the pan. Add the garlic and sweat. Deglaze with beef stock. Add the lemon juice and the gravy powder, mix everything, and bring to a boil briefly. Stir in the sour cream, season with salt and pepper to taste, and add the meatballs to the sauce along with the raclette cheese. Wait a few minutes until the meatballs are warm and the cheese begins to melt, then serve promptly.

4 SERVINGS

For the meatballs:

Activated charcoal tablets

1.35 pounds ground elk meat, or, alternatively, ground beef

3 heaping tablespoons breadcrumbs

1 egg

1 shallot, finely diced

2 tablespoons mustard (medium-hot)

Salt, pepper

1 pinch nutmeg

2 tablespoons butter

For the sauce:

9 ounces onions, finely chopped

1 clove garlic, finely chopped

⅔ cup beef stock

1 tablespoon lemon juice

2 tablespoons brown gravy powder

2 tablespoons sour cream

Salt, pepper

5.25 ounces raclette cheese, cut into pieces

BEAN AND BACON SOUP

DIFFICULTY
Apprentice

PREP TIME
10 minutes

COOKING TIME
approx. 2 hours

I. Melt the butter in a large saucepan at medium heat. Add the onion and sauté until translucent. Add the ham or bacon and sear on all sides (1 to 2 minutes). Add the beef to the pot and sear on all sides (2 to 3 minutes). Add the mirepoix, mix everything, and sauté for 2 to 3 minutes. Deglaze with the beef stock and pour in the water.

II. Add the potatoes and string beans to the pot. Season with the savory, tarragon, celery salt, pepper, and sugar and add the bay leaves. Bring to a boil, reduce the heat and simmer, stirring occasionally, for about 120 minutes or until the beef cubes fall apart on their own.

III. Season the stew with herb vinegar, if you like, and fold in the finely chopped parsley just before serving.

TIP

Like most stews, this one tastes especially delicious when properly steeped. So it's best prepared the night before, then warm it up again the next day to serve!

10 SERVINGS

1 tablespoon butter

1 large onion, finely chopped

7 ounces diced ham or bacon, cut into small, thin strips

1 pound beef (e.g., roast beef, shank, or chuck), cut into bite-sized cubes

1 bunch mirepoix (celery, carrots, leeks), finely sliced

Just over 2 cups beef stock

4¼ cups water

1½ pounds potatoes (floury), finely diced

2 pounds string beans (frozen or canned)

2 tablespoons savory

2 tablespoons tarragon

2 tablespoons celery salt

1 tablespoon pepper

1 pinch sugar

2 bay leaves

2 to 4 tablespoons herb vinegar

2 tablespoons parsley, finely chopped, to taste

TO THIS
(NEXT DISHES)

MASHED PEAS

DIFFICULTY
Apprentice

PREP TIME
5 minutes

PREPARATION
20 minutes

I. Heat the butter and olive oil in a pan over medium heat. Add the onions and sauté for 3 to 4 minutes.

II. Add the peas to the pan, reserving some for the garnish. Add the vegetable stock and mint, mix, and cook for 5 to 6 minutes.

III. Add the soy cream and simmer for 1 minute. Purée using an immersion blender, but not too finely. Season to taste with salt and freshly ground black pepper.

IV. Serve garnished with peas and fresh cress.

4 SERVINGS

¾ tablespoon butter

1 tablespoon olive oil

3.5 ounces onions, finely chopped

16 ounces frozen peas, thawed

1 brimming cup vegetable stock

Fresh mint, very finely chopped

⅓ cup soy cream

Salt

Freshly ground black pepper

Fresh cress, for garnish

DIREWOLF BREAD

DIFFICULTY
Apprentice

PREP TIME
1 hour
incl. resting time

COOKING TIME
11 to 13 minutes

I. Using the stencils on page 156 (or stencils found online), print out the outlines, glue them to cardboard, and cut them out.

II. In a bowl, thoroughly mix the flour, baking soda, ginger, cinnamon, nutmeg, and cocoa powder. Add the butter and work through with a mixer until a fine crumbly dough forms.

III. Stir in the brown sugar and salt.

IV. In a separate bowl, whisk the egg with molasses and add to the rest of the ingredients. Mix everything together and knead until smooth with your hands. Wrap the dough tightly and as airtight as possible in plastic wrap and place in the refrigerator for 30 minutes.

V. In the meantime, preheat the oven to 355°F and line two baking sheets with parchment paper.

VI. Roll out the dough on a lightly floured work surface to a thickness of about ½ an inch. Place the stencils on the dough and use a small, sharp knife to trace the outlines. Place the individual "loaves" on the prepared baking sheets and add details with a knife as desired. Bake for 11 to 13 minutes.

10 TO 20 PIECES DEPENDING ON THE STENCIL SIZE

½ cup plus 2 tablespoons flour

1 teaspoon baking soda

2 teaspoons ground ginger

1 teaspoon cinnamon

1 pinch nutmeg

1 tablespoon cocoa powder

½ cup butter

2 tablespoons brown sugar

1 pinch salt

1 egg

4 tablespoons molasses

Also needed:

Direwolf stencils (see page 156)

TIP

If the direwolf breads get too hard, store in a cookie jar with an apple slice for 2 to 3 days. This will make the bread softer again.

SAND SNAKE CHICKPEAS

DIFFICULTY
Apprentice

PREP TIME
5 minutes

COOKING TIME
15 to 20 minutes

I. Pat the chickpeas dry with paper towels. In a bowl, mix together with the canola oil, salt, paprika, turmeric, caraway, and cumin. Heat a nonstick pan over medium heat.

II. Add the chickpeas and roast for 15 to 20 minutes; do not stir, but toss the pan to keep the chickpeas as intact as possible. As soon as the chickpeas are golden brown and crispy, place them on a plate with paper towels to drain and allow to cool slightly before serving.

III. Serve garnished with a lemon wedge.

2 TO 3 SERVINGS

1½ cups chickpeas (canned), drained

4 tablespoons canola oil

2 teaspoons salt

2 teaspoons sweet paprika

2 teaspoons turmeric

2 teaspoons ground caraway

2 teaspoons ground cumin

Lemon wedges, for garnish

LORD COMMANDER'S BUTTERED TURNIPS

DIFFICULTY
Apprentice

PREP TIME
15 minutes

COOKING TIME
2½ hours

I. Wash and clean the rutabagas. Trim the ends on both sides with a sharp knife to let the beets stand better. Then use a large, sharp knife to cut them vertically into eight equally sized triangles, but not all the way down, so that the rutabagas still hang together at the bottom, like a flower opening (see picture). Leave the bowl in place.

II. Preheat the oven to 375°F.

III. Put 8 tablespoons of butter in a small microwave-resistant bowl and melt in the microwave. Add the tarragon, garlic, capers, sugar, caraway seeds, and olive oil and mix well. Put the shallots and the rutabaga in a roasting pan. Pour the butter sauce over the rutabagas, making sure that the sauce also gets into the vegetables' crevices. Top each rutabaga with a pat of butter and sprinkle with the smoked paprika. Drizzle with a little olive oil and season to taste with crushed black pepper.

IV. Bake for 2 ½ hours in a preheated oven or until the rutabagas are tender and golden brown; drizzle regularly with the butter sauce from the roasting pan.

4 SERVINGS

4 rutabagas

8 tablespoons butter, plus 4 tablespoons, in pats

2 tablespoons tarragon

1 tablespoon garlic, finely chopped

2 tablespoons capers (jar), drained

1 teaspoon sugar

1 tablespoon caraway seeds

2 tablespoons olive oil, plus a little more to drizzle

5 shallots, roughly chopped

1 tablespoon smoked paprika

Crushed black pepper, to taste

GREGOR CLEGANE'S SMASHED POTATOES

DIFFICULTY
Apprentice

PREP TIME
30 minutes

COOKING TIME
15 to 20 minutes

I. Wash the potatoes and place in a large pot of heavily salted water. Bring to a boil over medium heat and simmer for 20 to 25 minutes or until potatoes are tender.

II. Preheat the oven to 350°F. Line a baking sheet with parchment paper.

III. Tilt the cooked potatoes to drip and let drain for 5 minutes. Place on the prepared baking sheet and mash with the bottom of a heavy pan or skillet. Put one butter pat on each potato and sprinkle with smoked paprika and black pepper, to taste. Bake in the preheated oven for 15 to 20 minutes until golden brown.

IV. In the meantime, melt 1 tablespoon butter in a nonstick pan over medium heat. Sear the bacon strips on both sides and place on a plate lined with paper towels to drain. Let cool and then finely crumble or chop.

V. In a small bowl, whisk together the Greek yogurt and lime juice and refrigerate until ready to use.

VI. Once the potatoes are done, remove from the oven and place on a serving plate. Season with sea salt and black pepper to taste. Sprinkle with the crumbled bacon and fried onions and drizzle generously with the lime yogurt. Serve garnished with some fresh dill.

4 SERVINGS

10 medium-sized potatoes (preferably red)

Salt

½ cup butter, plus 1 tablespoon to cook the bacon

1 tablespoon smoked paprika powder

Black pepper

3.5 ounces bacon strips

3 ounces Greek yogurt

3 tablespoons lime juice

Fried onions (preprepared), for garnish

Sea salt

Fresh dill, for garnish

HONEYED LOCUSTS

DIFFICULTY
Apprentice

PREP TIME
5 minutes

I. Whisk together the olive oil, thyme, lemon juice, salt, and honey in a small bowl until the honey is completely dissolved.

II. Place the spice mixture in a nonstick pan and heat over medium heat, stirring regularly. Add the locusts and gently coat with the honey seasoning. Remove immediately and place on a plate lined with paper towels to drain. Let dry for a few minutes.

III. Store in an airtight sealable container and serve as an exotic snack.

4 SERVINGS

3 tablespoons olive oil

1 thyme sprig

Juice of ¼ lemon

1 pinch salt

4 tablespoons honey

1.5 ounces dried migratory locusts

TIP
You can get the dried locusts in organic/health food shops or online!

QYBURN'S WILDFIRE GUACAMOLE

DIFFICULTY
Apprentice

PREP TIME
10 minutes

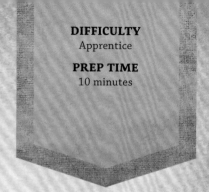

I. Carefully halve the avocados horizontally and remove the pit. Scoop the inside out of the skin with a spoon and mash the flesh roughly with a fork in a bowl. Roughly chop two of the chilis.

II. Cut the third chili into fine rings and save for garnish.

III. Place the tomatoes, shallot, lime juice, garlic, both diced chilies, and the yogurt in the bowl with the avocado purée and mix thoroughly. (If you prefer finer, use an immersion blender.) Season to taste with salt, pepper, and a dash of Tabasco. Cover with plastic wrap and chill in the refrigerator until ready to use.

IV. Flambé the nachos with the culinary torch to "char" them. Make sure they don't get too dark!

V. Stir the guacamole thoroughly again before dressing. Garnish generously with the chili rings and serve with nacho chips.

10 TO 12 SERVINGS

4 medium-sized, ripe avocados

3 red chilis

2 tomatoes, very finely diced

½ shallot, finely chopped

Juice of ½ lime

2 cloves garlic, very finely chopped or pressed

1 tablespoon natural yogurt

Salt

Freshly ground black pepper

1 dash Tabasco

Nacho chips, to taste

Also needed:

Culinary torch (optional)

TIP

Mix the avocado pits into your guacamole when storing it in the fridge to prevent it from turning ugly brown!

PAN BREAD

DIFFICULTY
Apprentice

PREP TIME
20 minutes
incl. resting time

Cooking Time
60 minutes

I. Carefully mix the flour and baking powder in a small bowl.

II. In a separate bowl, whisk together the yogurt, water, olive oil, and salt and add to the flour. Mix everything together thoroughly to form a soft, smooth dough. Let the dough rest for 15 minutes, then divide the dough into 10 portions.

III. Melt some butter in a hot pan, add a portion of dough and slightly flatten. Bake the pan bread until golden brown on all sides (2 to 3 minutes per side). To drain, place on a plate lined with paper towels and repeat with the remaining dough.

10 PIECES

1¾ cup plus 2 tablespoons flour

1 teaspoon baking powder

3.5 ounces Greek natural yogurt

½ cup water

1 tablespoon olive oil

1 teaspoon salt

Butter for baking

THEREAFTER

THE CHAINLESS MAESTER'S APPLE PIELETS

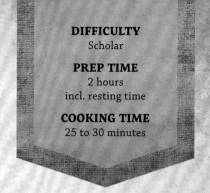

DIFFICULTY
Scholar

PREP TIME
2 hours
incl. resting time

COOKING TIME
25 to 30 minutes

I. Finely grate the ice-cold butter with a kitchen grater. Place in a mixing bowl and knead together with the cottage cheese, flour, sugar, and salt to form a smooth, supple dough. Wrap in plastic wrap and put in the refrigerator for 30 minutes.

II. Roll out the chilled dough into a rectangle on a lightly floured work surface. Fold over ⅓ of the dough on one side, then the other. Turn the dough 90 degrees, roll it out again, and fold it over again as described before. Wrap in plastic film and let rest again in the refrigerator for 1 hour.

III. In the meantime, prepare the filling. To do so, peel, core, and dice the apples.

IV. Melt the butter in a saucepan over medium heat and add the apples. Sprinkle with cane sugar and let caramelize slightly. Then add the lemon juice and 2 tablespoons water and steam the apples for about 2 to 3 minutes or until they are almost soft.

V. Mix 3 tablespoons of water with the cornstarch in a cup and add to the boiling apple mixture. Mix well, boil briefly, and remove from the stove. Stir in the vanilla extract, cinnamon, and lemon zest and let cool for a few minutes.

VI. Meanwhile, preheat the oven to 390°F. Grease the tin with butter.

VII. Roll out the dough on a floured work surface to a thickness of about ⅕ of an inch. Using a round cutter, about ¾ of an inch larger than the tart molds, cut out the dough circles. (Alternatively, use a large glass.) Line the molds with the dough circles and carefully press down on the bottom and sides. Cut off any excess dough with a knife, fill in with the apple mixture, and smooth the top.

VIII. Briefly knead the leftover dough, roll out, and cut into strips about 4¾ inches long. Lay the strips of dough over the filling in a lattice pattern (see picture) and gently press down on the edge.

IX. In a small bowl, mix the egg yolk with the remaining 2 tablespoons of water and brush the strips of dough generously with it. Bake on the middle rack for about 25 to 30 minutes, until golden brown.

6 SERVINGS

For the dough:

½ cup butter, ice cold

9 ounces low-fat cottage cheese

2 cups pastry flour

1 tablespoon sugar

1 pinch of salt

For the Filling:

5 tart apples (½ pound)

2¾ tablespoons butter, plus a little more for greasing the baking pans

4 tablespoons cane sugar

4 tablespoons lemon juice

7 tablespoons water

2¾ tablespoons cornstarch

1 teaspoon vanilla extract

1 pinch ground cinnamon

1 teaspoon lemon zest

1 egg yolk

Also needed:

6 tart molds (about 5 inches across), round cookie cutter (about 5.5 inches across)

WINE-POACHED PEARS

DIFFICULTY
Apprentice

PREP TIME
5 minutes

COOKING TIME
20 minutes

I. Wash the lemon in hot water, pat dry with paper towels, and cut into slices.

II. Combine the red wine, sugar, and cinnamon stick in a saucepan. Add the lemon slices and bring to a boil over medium heat, simmering for 10 minutes.

III. During this time, peel the pears and remove the core from the bottom with a sharp knife. Remove the cinnamon stick and lemon slices and place the pears in the pot instead so that they are completely covered with the liquid. Put the lid on, reduce the heat, and simmer for about 10 minutes. Then remove from the stove and let cool a bit in the pan.

IV. Plate as desired and serve with a generous amount of the wine sauce. Best enjoyed lukewarm.

8 PIECES

1 organic lemon

3¼ cups red wine

¾ cup sugar

1 cinnamon stick

8 fresh pears (e.g., Bartlett)

ROYAL CREAM SWANS

DIFFICULTY
Maester

PREP TIME
1 hour

COOKING TIME
40 to 80 minutes

I. Preheat the oven, using the convection setting, to 215°F.

II. In a mixing bowl, beat the egg whites and flour with an electric hand-held mixer until soft peaks form. Gradually add the sugar and continue beating on medium speed until forming stiff peaks (about 5 minutes). Put the meringue into either a piping bag with a round tip or a freezer bag with the corner cut off.

III. Place the stencils under wax paper or baking paper and use the piping bag to trace the shape of the base, the wings, and the neck/head. Decorate each swan head with a peeled almond as a beak and touch up with a little more beaten egg white. Since meringue is extremely fragile and delicate, some parts may break later when serving. Pipe extra to have on hand if this happens. You need at least 6 to 8 bodies, 6 to 8 necks/heads, and 12 to 16 wings. If necessary, work with several baking sheets and make several batches.

IV. Carefully place the paper with the swan parts on a baking sheet and bake in the oven for 40 minutes. Warning: The necks finish faster than the other parts! Once the meringue is light, dry, and crispy, these pieces are done. Remove, let cool, and meanwhile bake the remaining "components" for another 40 minutes. Remove from the oven and let cool completely on the baking sheet. Then draw eyes on the heads with the black food pen.

V. To assemble the swans, place a meringue base on a serving plate. Arrange several scoops of ice cream using a small ice cream scoop so that the whole thing looks like the body of a swan (see picture). Using a wooden stick, poke a hole where the neck will go and carefully position it. Place the wings on the swan's left and right. Surround with a "sea" of pomegranate seeds and serve immediately.

6 TO 8 SERVINGS

6 egg whites

½ teaspoon flour

¾ cup fine sugar

5 peeled almonds

Black food coloring marker or pen

3 scoops vanilla ice cream

18 ounces pomegranate seeds, to taste

Also needed:

Swan stencil (see page 154)

DRAGON EGGS

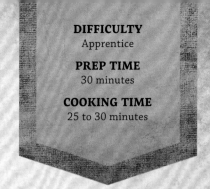

DIFFICULTY
Apprentice

PREP TIME
30 minutes

COOKING TIME
25 to 30 minutes

I. Preheat the oven to 350°F. Grease the silicone egg molds with butter.

II. In a bowl, cream the butter, sugar, vanilla extract, salt, and lemon juice using a hand mixer. Gradually and carefully add the eggs one by one and mix well.

III. In a separate bowl, mix the flour with the cornstarch and baking powder and, in batches, stir into the batter. Pour it all into the prepared silicone mold and bake for 25 to 30 minutes. Remove from the oven and let cool.

IV. Meanwhile put the cream in a saucepan and bring to a boil over medium heat. Remove immediately from the heat, add the chocolate, and stir until the chocolate has completely melted. Release the cooled eggs from the mold and coat the smooth surfaces with the chocolate to adhere both halves together.

V. If the chocolate has become too hard, put it in the microwave for a few seconds. Then brush the eggs all over with the chocolate and spread the almond slivers on top like scales (see picture). Allow the chocolate to set for a few minutes.

8 TO 10 PIECES

1 heaping cup butter, plus a little more for the mold

1 cup sugar

1 teaspoon vanilla extract

1 pinch salt

1 tablespoon lemon juice

4 eggs

1¾ cups flour

3.5 ounces cornstarch

1 teaspoon baking powder

¼ cup cream

10.5 ounces milk chocolate, roughly chopped

7 ounces sliced almonds

Also needed:

Silicone egg molds
(about 4 inches by 3 inches)

TIP

If you have more dough than silicone egg molds, simply repeat the process as often as needed!

ARYA'S PILFERED TARTLETS

DIFFICULTY
Apprentice

PREP TIME
25 minutes

COOKING TIME
20 minutes

I. Cut the parchment paper into twelve small squares measuring 5.5 by 5.5 inches. Place a square of parchment paper in the middle of each cup in the muffin tin and press the parchment paper into the cup using an appropriately sized glass. Press the resulting folds in the baking paper onto the sides of the depression.

II. Preheat the oven to 350°F.

III. Lightly beat the butter, sugar, lemon zest, and lemon juice together. Add the eggs one by one, beating well after adding each one.

IV. In a separate bowl, whisk together the flour, baking powder, and salt and add to the butter mixture in batches, alternating with the milk. Mix well. Pour the batter evenly into the prepared muffin tin, smooth the tops, and bake for 20 minutes or until a wooden skewer (or toothpick) inserted into the center of the muffin comes out clean. Remove from the oven and let cool completely.

V. In the meantime, prepare the frosting. To do this, lightly beat the butter with the powdered sugar, lemon zest, and lemon juice in a bowl. Then quickly fold in the mascarpone and generously spread the resulting cream over the muffins. Sprinkle with a little cinnamon if you like and garnish with a fresh raspberry.

12 PIECES

For the tartlets:

½ cup softened butter

½ cup sugar

2 teaspoons lemon zest

3 tablespoons lemon juice

2 eggs

1¾ cups flour

2 teaspoons baking powder

1 pinch salt

½ cup milk

For the frosting:

½ cup softened butter

⅞ cup powdered sugar

1 teaspoon lemon zest

2 teaspoons lemon juice

1 cup mascarpone

Cinnamon, to taste

12 fresh raspberries, for garnish

Also needed:

12-cup muffin tin

THE RED WOMAN'S TRIFLE

DIFFICULTY
Apprentice

PREP TIME
40 minutes

COOKING TIME
35 to 40 minutes

Prepare the cake crumbs:

I. Preheat the oven, using the convection setting, to 350°F. Grease the pan with butter and line with baking paper.

II. In a bowl, thoroughly mix the flour with the cocoa powder, baking powder, and baking soda.

III. In a mixing bowl, beat the softened butter with the sugar, vanilla extract, and salt until light and creamy. Work the eggs, one by one, into the butter mixture.

IV. Whisk the buttermilk vigorously with the oil, vinegar, and food coloring in a separate bowl.

V. Sift the flour mixture into the butter mixture, then add the buttermilk mixture. Whisk together until a smooth dough forms. Pour into prepared baking pan, smooth the tops, and bake for 35 to 40 minutes or until a wooden skewer (or toothpick) inserted into center of cake comes out clean. Remove from the oven and let cool completely in the pan. Crumble coarsely into a bowl.

To prepare the lemon cottage cheese:

VI. In a small bowl, whip the heavy cream with the vanilla extract until stiff and refrigerate until ready to use.

VII. Wash the lemon with hot water and dry. Use a grater to grate the yellow peel. Halve the lemon and juice it.

VIII. In a separate bowl, whisk the cottage cheese until smooth. Add the sugar, lemon zest, and lemon juice and mix. Fold the whipped cream into the cottage cheese, season to taste, and add a little more sugar if necessary. Chill in the refrigerator until ready to use.

Continued on the following page...

8 SERVINGS

For the cake crumbs:

¼ cup soft butter plus a little more for greasing the baking pan

1 cup flour

2 teaspoons cocoa powder

1 teaspoon baking powder

½ teaspoon baking soda

¾ cup sugar

½ teaspoon vanilla extract

½ pinch salt

2 eggs

½ cup buttermilk, room temperature

¼ cup vegetable oil

½ tablespoon apple cider vinegar

Red food coloring, depending on the desired color intensity

For the lemon cottage cheese:

⅔ cup whipping cream

2 teaspoons vanilla extract

1 medium organic lemon

1 pound cottage cheese

3 tablespoons sugar

Prepare the raspberry sauce:

IX. Place the raspberries in a saucepan with the sugar and a squeeze of lemon juice. Mash the berries a little with a fork, bring to a boil over low heat, stirring occasionally, and simmer for 5 minutes. Then strain through a sieve to remove the seeds and allow the fruit sauce to cool.

Serve the trifle:

X. Alternately layer the cake crumbs, lemon curd, and raspberry sauce in tall serving glasses, if desired. Finish with the cottage cheese and top off with more sauce. Garnish each with a fresh raspberry. Refrigerate until ready to serve.

For the raspberry sauce:

1 pound raspberries

3 to 4 tablespoons sugar

1 dash of lemon juice

8 fresh raspberries, for garnish

Also needed:

Baking pan (about 11.5 inches across)

SUGAR DOUGHNUTS

DIFFICULTY
Apprentice

PREP TIME
30 minutes + about
13 hours resting time

COOKING TIME
20 to 25 minutes

Prepare the starter dough:

I. Put the water in a bowl and crumble in the yeast.

II. Stir until the yeast has completely dissolved and sift the flour into the bowl. Mix everything together. Cover with a clean tea towel and let rest at room temperature for at least 12 hours.

Prepare the main dough:

III. Put the lukewarm water in a bowl and crumble in the yeast. Stir until the yeast has completely dissolved.

IV. Mix the dough starter, flour, olive oil, sugar, and yeast water in a mixing bowl and knead gently for at least 10 minutes.

V. Then cover the dough with a clean tea towel and let rest for 30 minutes. After resting, divide the dough into ten equal portions. Form into balls and let rest covered with a clean tea towel for 10 minutes. On a lightly floured work surface, shape the dough balls into strands about 14 inches long. Join both ends of the dough strands and press firmly together.

VI. Prepare a bowl of lukewarm water and a bowl of sesame seeds. Lay out two sheets of parchment paper. Horizontally dip the dough rings halfway into the water and then dip this moistened half into the bowl of sesame seeds.

Continued on the following page...

10 SERVINGS

For the starter dough:

1¼ cups water

½ teaspoon fresh yeast

2 cups whole wheat bread flour

For the main dough:

Just over ⅓ cup lukewarm water, plus a bowl

2 teaspoon yeast for the starter dough

2 cups whole wheat bread flour

2 tablespoons olive oil

2 tablespoons sugar

7 ounces sesame seeds

VII. Place on the parchment paper with the sesame side facing up (five rings per sheet). Cover with a clean tea towel and rest for another 30 minutes.

VIII. Meanwhile, put a baking sheet in the oven, place a heat-resistant bowl with a little water in it at the bottom of the oven, and preheat the oven to 425°F. Once the oven is preheated, place the parchment paper on the baking sheet and bake for 20 to 25 minutes until golden brown. Then remove the doughnuts from the oven and place on a wire rack to cool.

BLOOD RED WEDDING CAKE

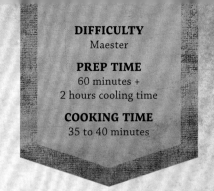

DIFFICULTY
Maester

PREP TIME
60 minutes +
2 hours cooling time

COOKING TIME
35 to 40 minutes

Preparing the cake bases:

I. Preheat the oven, using the convection setting, to 350°F. Grease both baking molds with butter and line with baking parchment.

II. In a bowl, thoroughly mix the flour with the baking cocoa, baking powder, and baking soda. In a mixing bowl, beat the softened butter with the sugar, vanilla extract, and salt until light and creamy. Work the eggs, one by one, into the butter mixture.

III. Whisk the buttermilk vigorously with the oil, vinegar, and food coloring in a separate bowl.

IV. Sift the flour mixture into the butter mixture, and then add the buttermilk mixture. Whisk together until a smooth dough forms. Pour into the prepared baking pans, smooth off the tops, and bake for 35 to 40 minutes or until a wooden skewer (or toothpick) inserted into the center of the cake base comes out clean. Then remove from the oven and let cool completely in the pan before releasing. In the meantime, prepare the frosting.

Prepare the frosting:

V. Put the butter in a bowl and sift the powdered sugar over it. Add the vanilla extract and whip until light and fluffy. Then add the cream cheese and stir in.

Continued on the following page...

8 SERVINGS

For the cake base:

½ cup soft butter, plus more for greasing the baking pan

1¾ cup plus 2 tablespoons flour

4 teaspoons baking cocoa

2 teaspoons baking powder

1 teaspoon baking soda

1½ cups sugar

1 teaspoon vanilla extract

1 pinch salt

3 eggs

1 cup buttermilk, room temperature

½ cup vegetable oil

1 tablespoon apple cider vinegar

Red food coloring, depending on the desired color intensity

For the frosting:

1 heaping cup soft butter at room temperature

1¼ cups powdered sugar

1 teaspoon vanilla extract

14 ounces room temperature cream cheese

2 tablespoons milk for soaking the cake base

Put the cake together:

VI. Once the cake bases have cooled, place one of the bottoms on the working surface and brush with some of the milk with a baking brush. Evenly spread a layer of cream cheese frosting on it and place the second cake base upside down (with the smooth side facing upward) on the frosting. Frost the cake with the remaining frosting and chill in the fridge for at least 2 hours. Meanwhile, prepare the "chocolate blood."

Prepare the "chocolate blood":

VII. Bring the cream to a boil in a small saucepan over medium heat, stirring regularly. Add the chocolate, remove from the heat, and let sit for 3 minutes until the chocolate has melted. Mix everything together carefully. Mix in the food coloring. Then let the ganache cool to room temperature.

VIII. Once the ganache has cooled, remove the cake from the fridge. Spread the "chocolate blood" with a spoon on the top of the cake and let it flow down the sides for the effect. Refrigerate until ready to serve.

For the "chocolate blood":

Just under ⅓ cup cream

3.5 ounces white chocolate, roughly chopped

1.5 ounces milk chocolate, roughly chopped

Red food coloring, depending on the desired color intensity

Also needed:

Two baking sheets
(about 8 inches across)

STUFFED BAKED APPLES

DIFFICULTY
Apprentice

PREP TIME
20 minutes

COOKING TIME
30 to 40 minutes

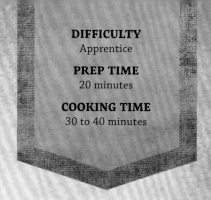

I. Wash the apples, cut off a horizontal "lid," and remove the core with an apple corer.

II. Preheat the oven, using the convection setting, to 355°F.

III. In a bowl, mix the almonds with the raisins, maple syrup, and the cinnamon. Add the marzipan and mix. Fill the apples with the mixture, place in a mold/casserole dish with sufficient space between them, and spread the butter pieces over them. Place the tops of the apples on a piece of aluminum foil and set aside. Cook in the preheated oven for 30 to 40 minutes.

IV. In the meantime, prepare the vanilla sauce. To do this, remove 3 to 4 tablespoons of the milk and stir in a small bowl with the cornstarch until smooth. Cut the vanilla pod in half lengthwise, carefully scrape out the seeds with a knife, and bring the pod and the rest of the milk to a boil in a small saucepan. Remove from the stove.

V. Whisk together the milk-cornstarch mixture and the egg yolks, then stir into the vanilla milk and heat, stirring constantly, until the sauce becomes creamy. Don't cook! Season to taste with the remaining maple syrup and let cool slightly while stirring occasionally.

VI. Remove the baked apples from the oven, arrange on plates, garnish with warm vanilla sauce, put on the apple tops, and serve immediately.

4 SERVINGS

For the baked apples:

4 tart apples (e.g., Rhode Island Greening, Granny Smith, etc.)

1.25 ounces sliced almonds

3 teaspoons raisins

1 tablespoon maple syrup

1 pinch ground cinnamon

1¾ ounces raw marzipan, finely chopped

1½ tablespoons butter in pats

For the vanilla sauce:

1 cup milk

1 teaspoon cornstarch

1 vanilla bean

3 egg yolks

2 tablespoons maple syrup

Also needed:

Corer

SNOWBALLS

DIFFICULTY
Apprentice

PREP TIME
10 minutes

COOLING TIME
3 hours

I. In a small bowl, carefully mix 3.5 ounces grated coconut with the condensed milk and chill in the refrigerator for 3 hours.

II. Use a tablespoon to scoop out the coconut mixture and, with slightly moistened hands, evenly form into balls the size of ping-pong balls.

III. Put the remaining coconut into a small bowl and form into "snowballs." Place in an airtight container and refrigerate until ready to eat.

ABOUT 20 PIECES

3.5 ounces plus 1 ounce grated coconut

⅘ cup sweetened condensed milk

POMEGRANATE FIGS

DIFFICULTY
Apprentice

PREP TIME
5 minutes

I. Wash the figs, pat dry with paper towels, and quarter with a sharp small knife so they are still intact at the bottom. Gently squeeze the bottom half of the figs so they bloom open.

II. In a small bowl, blend the cream cheese and the lemon juice together.

III. Place 1 to 2 tablespoons of cream cheese in the middle of each fig, garnish with a few pomegranate seeds, and drizzle with honey. Serve immediately.

4 SERVINGS

4 ripe figs

3.5 ounces plain cream cheese

1 teaspoon lemon juice

Pomegranate seeds

Honey, to taste

SANSA'S LEMON CAKE

DIFFICULTY
Apprentice

PREP TIME
7 hours

COOKING TIME
20 minutes

I. Grate the zest from a lemon and squeeze out the juice. Cut the other two lemons into thin slices. Pour 1 cup water and 1 heaping cup sugar in a saucepan and bring to a boil over high heat. Reduce the temperature, add the lemon slices, and simmer for about 5 to 7 minutes. Then remove from the pan with a slotted spoon and let drain. Then spread the lemon slices slightly apart on a baking sheet lined with parchment paper and let dry at room temperature for 6 hours.

II. Preheat the oven to 375°F.

III. Add the ¾ cup sugar, eggs, and egg yolks into a large bowl and whisk. Add the sour cream and work it in thoroughly. Then add the lemon zest, lemon juice, and vanilla extract and mix together. Put the flour, baking powder, and a pinch of salt in the bowl and again work it through carefully. Then melt the butter, add to the dough, and stir in. Lastly, fold in the lemon jam.

IV. Thoroughly grease the cups of a 12-cup muffin tin. Place a dried lemon slice at the bottom of each cup, then pour in enough batter to fill about three-quarters full. Bake the lemon cakes in the preheated oven for about 20 minutes.

V. After baking, let the cakes cool in the tin for 30 minutes. Then turn the muffin tin over and carefully tip it onto the work surface. (The lemon cakes should pop out of the pan fairly easily.) Allow to cool a little longer, then serve warm.

FOR 12 CAKES

3 organic lemons

1 cup water

1 heaping cup sugar

¾ cup sugar for boiling

2 eggs

1 egg yolk

¼ cup sour cream

1 teaspoon vanilla extract

1 cup flour

2 level teaspoons baking powder

1 pinch of salt

½ cup butter, plus more for greasing the muffin tin

3 tablespoons lemon jam

WINTER CAKE

DIFFICULTY
Apprentice

PREP TIME
30 minutes
incl. cooling time

COOKING TIME
50 minutes

I. Preheat the oven to 355°F. Grease the baking pan with butter and sprinkle with a little flour.

II. In a mixing bowl, using a mixer, cream the butter with the sugar, vanilla extract, and salt until light. Then, one by one, work in the eggs. In a separate bowl, mix the flour, baking powder, cocoa powder, and cinnamon.

III. Add the red wine and the butter mixture to the dry ingredients and stir together carefully. Stir in the chocolate.

IV. Pour into the prepared pan, smooth off the top, and bake for about 50 minutes or until a toothpick or wooden skewer inserted into the center of the cake comes out clean. Then remove from the oven and let cool in the pan for 10 minutes. Carefully turn the cake out of the mold and let cool completely.

V. To serve, sprinkle generously with powdered sugar.

1 PIECE

2¼ sticks softened butter, plus more for greasing the pan

2 cups cake flour, plus a little more for the pan

1 cup sugar

1 teaspoon vanilla extract

1 pinch salt

4 eggs

1 teaspoon baking powder

3 tablespoons cocoa powder

1 teaspoon cinnamon

½ cup red wine

3.5 ounces dark chocolate, chopped

Powdered sugar, for sprinkling

Also needed:

Baking pan with tube
(about 12 inches across)

STUFFED PEACHES

DIFFICULTY
Apprentice

PREP TIME
5 minutes

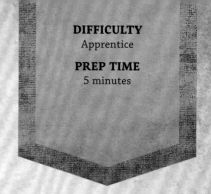

I. Wash, clean, and drain the strawberries. Mix together in a bowl with the sugar and vanilla extract and purée finely. Add the cottage cheese to the strawberry puree and mix carefully. Chill until ready to use.

II. Wash and clean the peaches and dry with paper towels. Halve horizontally with a sharp knife and deseed. Fill the peach halves with a generous dollop of strawberry cottage cheese and garnish with cranberries and lemon zest, as desired. Serve immediately!

4 SERVINGS

9 ounces fresh strawberries

1½ tablespoons sugar

1 teaspoon vanilla extract

½ pound Cottage cheese

4 fresh peaches

Dried cranberries, for garnish

TIP

Enjoy the rest of the strawberry cottage cheese as is or use it for other recipes!

THE WHITE WALKER

DIFFICULTY
Apprentice

PREP TIME
10 minutes

FREEZING TIME
60 minutes

I. Place the yogurt, cream, sugar, and lemon juice in a mixing bowl and work through with a hand blender until the sugar has completely dissolved.

II. Place the mixture in the ice cream machine and freeze for about 60 minutes according to the equipment instructions.

III. Separate some of the ice cream into a small bowl and mix with the Blue Curaçao until the ice cream is marbeled blue. Fold the marbled ice cream into the rest of the ice cream to create blue streaks throughout. If necessary, chill the ice cream briefly in the freezer.

IV. To serve, scoop ice cream into a bowl and drizzle generously with cherry syrup.

4 SERVINGS

1²/₅ cups natural yogurt

³/₄ cup cream

1 cup icing sugar

1 tablespoon lemon juice

20 ml Blue Curaçao (non-alcoholic)

Cherry syrup (store-bought), to taste

Also required:

Ice cream machine

DRINKS

ARBOR GOLD

DIFFICULTY
Apprentice

PREP TIME
5 minutes

RESTING TIME
3 to 4 weeks

I. Put the honey in the large sealable (carefully rinsed) container. Pour in the vodka and stir until the honey has completely dissolved. Then add the cinnamon stick, vanilla bean, cardamom pod, cinnamon buds, and cloves, close the container carefully, and leave in a cool, dark place for 3 to 4 weeks. Shake vigorously every few days.

II. Strain the finished liqueur through a fine sieve and pour into the 1-liter bottle previously washed in hot water. Discard the spices. Close the bottle tightly and shake well. Enjoy slightly chilled.

III. Arbor Gold keeps for at least 2 to 3 months.

ABOUT 1 L ARBOR GOLD

17.5 ounces blossom honey

3¼ cups vodka

1 cinnamon stick

1 vanilla bean

1 cardamom pod

Cinnamon buds, to taste

1 to 2 cloves

Also needed:

Sealable bottle or container with a 1.5 L capacity, sealable bottle with a 1 L capacity

TIP

The longer the honey liqueur steeps, the more delicious it tastes!

LORD COMMANDER'S HOT CHOCOLATE

DIFFICULTY
Apprentice

PREP TIME
10 minutes

COOKING TIME
5 minutes

I. In a mixing bowl, with a hand mixer, whip the cream until stiff.

II. Heat the milk, cocoa, vanilla extract, and dark chocolate in a saucepan over medium-high heat, stirring continuously until the chocolate is completely melted. Make sure that it doesn't start to boil! Reduce heat if needed.

III. Remove the pot from the heat and let cool for 2 to 3 minutes. Then stir again thoroughly and pour into two mugs or heat-resistant glasses. Garnish with whipped cream as desired and sprinkle with chocolate shavings. Serve immediately.

2 SERVINGS

¼ cup cream

Just over 2 cups milk

2 tablespoons unsweetened cocoa

1 teaspoon vanilla extract

3 ounces dark chocolate, roughly chopped

Whipped cream, for garnish

Chocolate Shavings, for garnish

TYROSHI'S PEAR BRANDY

DIFFICULTY
Apprentice

PREP TIME
10 minutes

RESTING TIME
4 weeks

I. Wash, peel, and quarter the pears. Remove the core and dice the fruit.

II. Halve the vanilla bean lengthwise and scrape out the seeds with a small, sharp knife.

III. Place the diced pears, sugar, and vanilla in a sufficiently large, sealable, clean, and rinsed container and pour in the alcohol. Mix everything together and close the jar carefully. Leave in a warm, preferably sunny place for at least 4 weeks. Shake every few days.

IV. Then strain the pear brandy through a sieve or cheesecloth. Squeeze out the pear pieces and discard along with the vanilla. Pour the brandy into a clean, preferably sterilized bottle and store in a cool, dark place. Enjoy in moderation!

3¼ CUPS BRANDY

4 pears

1¼ cups sugar

1 vanilla bean

3 cups vodka

Also needed:

Sealable jar with a capacity of 1.5 liters, bottle with a capacity of 25 fl ounces

SEKANJABIN

DIFFICULTY
Apprentice

PREP TIME
5 minutes

COOKING TIME
50 minutes

I. Place the water and sugar in a heavy-bottomed saucepan and heat over a medium heat, stirring constantly until the sugar is completely dissolved. Reduce the heat and simmer gently for 10 to 15 minutes.

II. Add the apple cider vinegar and leave to simmer for another 30 minutes or until the mixture is slightly thickened. Taste and season with vinegar as desired, depending on how sweet you like it. Add the lime juice and stir.

III. Remove some beautiful leaves from the mint to garnish. Add the rest to the pot and let simmer for 3 to 4 minutes. Then remove from the stove and let cool completely. Chill in the refrigerator until ready to use.

IV. To serve, wash the cucumber, pat dry with paper towels, and peel with a vegetable peeler or zest cutter so that you get long, narrow strips. Place a few strips of cucumber peel in each jar.

V. Remove the mint from the Sekanjabin, pour into the glasses, and serve each garnished with a mint leaf.

7 TO 8 SERVINGS

Just over 2 cups of water

2 cups sugar

½ cup apple cider vinegar

1 dash lime juice

½ bunch fresh mint

1 cucumber

TIP

If you prefer your Sekanjabin a bit crisper—and less sweet—you can also top it up with mineral water or lemonade!

CERSEI'S BLOODY SANGRIA

DIFFICULTY
Apprentice

PREP TIME
15 minutes

RESTING TIME
2 to 3 hours

I. Halve the melon and cut out balls with a melon baller.

II. Place the red wine, orange liqueur, melon balls, lime slices, star fruit slices, and mango cubes in a sufficiently large jug or other container and mix well. Chill in the refrigerator for at least 2 to 3 hours. For serving, pour some crushed ice into a glass, add the sangria with the desired amount of fruit, and top up with lemonade to taste.

III. Serve garnished with a blood orange slice.

5 TO 6 SERVINGS

1 small honeydew melon

3 cups red wine (dry)

½ cup orange liqueur

1 lime, cut into thin slices

1 star fruit, thinly sliced

1 mango, cubed

Crushed ice (optional)

Lemonade, to taste

1 blood orange, thinly sliced

Also needed:

Melon baller

ICED MILK
AND HONEY

DIFFICULTY
Apprentice

PREP TIME
5 minutes

PREPARATION
10 minutes

I. Place the ice cream bowls in the freezer.

II. Place the milk, salt, and chopped walnuts in a medium-sized saucepan and bring to a boil over medium heat, stirring constantly. Add the honey and simmer until the honey has completely dissolved. Remove from the stove and let cool completely. Chill in the refrigerator until ready to serve.

III. To serve, take the ice cream bowls out of the freezer, place a scoop of walnut ice cream in each bowl, and top with the honey milk. Sprinkle with chopped pistachios to taste. Serve immediately

4 SERVINGS

3¼ cups milk

1 pinch salt

1.75 ounces walnuts, very finely chopped

2 tablespoons honey

4 scoops walnut ice cream

Finely chopped pistachios, for garnish

Also needed:

4 ice cream bowls or cups

ACKNOWLEDGMENTS

Okay, the work is done. The dishes are cooked, the photos taken, the recipes written. Time to light the fireplace, pour a glass of good red wine, and get a bit more personal.

The works of George R. R. Martin have always been at the forefront of my list of absolute favorite books. From *A Song of Ice and Fire* to *Tales of Dunk and Egg*, his terrific works enchant and captivate millions, creating worlds that would later get brought to life on screen through *Game of Thrones* and the all-new HBO series *House of the Dragon*. For me, there's nothing quite like sitting here in the firelight while the wind whips the treetops outside the window, opening up a book by G. R. R. M. to enjoy his cool poetic tapestry and later on to watch on the screen what talented media makers like David Benioff, D. B. White, Ryan J. Condal, and Jane Goldman made it.

Who doesn't remember Ned Stark's shocking departure in Game of Thrones? The Red Wedding? The fate of Shireen Baratheon at the stake? Of the Battle of Hartheim and all the other unforgettable scenes, characters, and moments that George R. R. Martin has bestowed upon

us? How ingenious must one be to come up with a twist as brilliant as Hodor's, and how patient to play that card after twenty solid years of holding a full house in your hand? Seriously: No other twist in literary history has ever impressed me more than this one.

Hodor...

Hold the door... simply unbelievable.

Anyhow, we've come to the end and that means it's time to look back and review the last few months. Let's not beat around the bush: The gods haven't been kind to me lately. I have no idea what I did to them, but especially in the final phase of this project I had to contend with some difficulties. That, in itself, is nothing new to me. Stating as much without any self-pity, life has never made it easy for me. This time, however, Lady Fortuna wore combat boots—teel-toed... and damn, can she kick hard! But as the saying so aptly goes: What doesn't kill us only makes us stronger. Ask Tyrion Lannister. Or Theon Graufreud. They know what I'm talking about.

Everything I have achieved (and will ever achieve) is due to discipline, hard work—and a handful of wonderful people without whom you would not be able to hold this book in your hands.

First and foremost, I would like to thank my publishing team at DK, especially Monika Schlitzer, who brought this project over the finish line with enthusiasm, vision, and a steady hand. But also Doreen Wolff, Heike Fassbender, Carmen Brand, Nicole Walter, and all the other good souls who always stood by my side to help with words and deeds. In addition, my sincere thanks (in no particular order): Dimitrie Harder, my "Partner in Crime," who captures in pictures all the crazy ideas that spew through my head; Jo Löffler and Holger Tom Grimm "Holle" Wiest, without whom nothing would be the way it is, even after all these years; Roberts "Rob" Urlovski, my "just-in-case man," for whom the same applies; Ulrich "the Plague" Pest, my best friend, who means more to me than he will ever imagine; Thomas and Alexa Stamm, I'm full of sincere gratitude for all that they have done for me; my "Brother from Another Mother" Thomas Böhm, along with Gabi, Susi, and Tommy; Tobias, Andrea, Lea, Finja, and this guy she's been sharing the shack with for a while, Jannik or Jannis or something; Katharina "The Only True Cat" Böhm; Annelies Haubold; and in memoriam, the incomparable, unforgettable Oskar "Ossi" Böhm, who was taken from these parts far too early; and last, but not least, my family, who give me the opportunity to experience great adventures like this again and again. For everything you like about this book, thank these people. For all the mistakes, inaccuracies in the content, and too much lovage, however, you are welcome to parade me around in sackcloth and ashes. But don't forget: Flowers don't grow from nipped buds!

Tom Grimm

ABOUT THE AUTHOR
AND PHOTOGRAPHER

TOM GRIMM

Tom Grimm, born in 1972, has worked as an author, translator, journalist, editor, producer, and publisher for a large number of international book and newspaper publishers since completing his bookseller apprenticeship. In addition to his enthusiasm for literature, film, and video games, his love goes above all to theme parks, trips, and barbecue experiments all year round. Recently, he was awarded the World Cookbook Award for his work. Together with his family, a pack of wild cats, and several life-size images of Batman, KungFuPanda, Rayman, and Thrall the Orc, he lives and works in a small town in the Wiehengebirge near Bielefeld, which despite all prophecies of doom still exists.

DIMITRIE HARDER

Dimitrie Harder was born second in 1977. He was born to a Russian mother and a German father in Kyrgyzstan (Central Asia), distinguished not only by its magnificent mountain panoramas and beautiful nature, but also by its culture interwoven with old myths and legends. In 1990 he came to Germany with his family, where he later discovered his passion for photography and turned his hobby into a career. With a lot of patience and attention to detail, he can put himself in almost any mood required by the worlds in which he moves with his photography. He loves biking, running, and hiking; hates food waste; and is the only person on earth who has ever officially referred to his "partner in crime," Tom Grimm, as a "lout."

RECIPE INDEX

SWEET

VEGETARIAN

RIGHT
WING

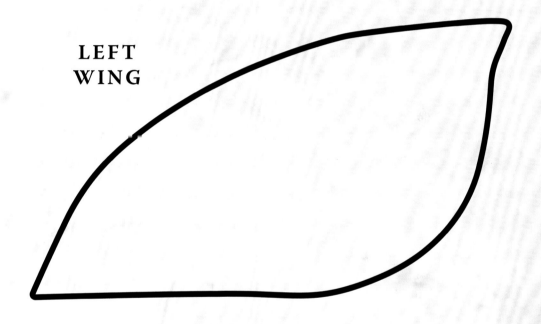

LEFT
WING

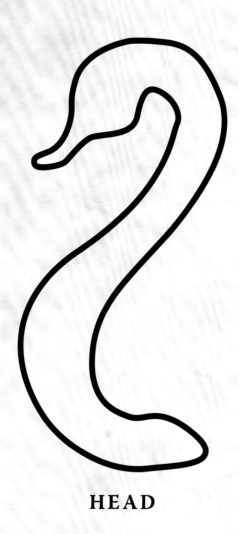

HEAD

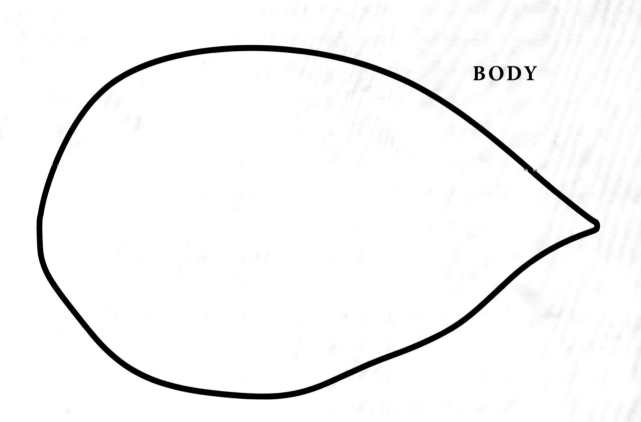

BODY

RECHTER
FLÜGEL

PO Box 15
Cobb, CA 95426

ISBN: 978-1-958862-10-0

Originally published as *Das inoffizielle House of the Dragon Kochbuch*, © 2022 DK
Verlag Dorling Kindersley. Created by Grinning Cat Productions.

Manufactured in China

10 9 8 7 6 5 4 3 2 1